First published in Great Britain in 1999 by
Element Children's Books
Shaftesbury Dorset SP7 8BP

Published in the USA in 1999 by
Element Books, Inc.
160 North Washington Street,
Boston MA 02114

Published in Australia in 1999 by
Element Books and distributed by
Penguin Australia Limited,
487 Maroondah Highway, Ringwood,
Victoria 3134

To my son Joe.
Lauren

To my mum, who threw me in at the deep end.
Zena

With special thanks to Kristin and Dave Sjøvorr-Packham and their beautiful waterbabies Anna and Lucy; the "Little Dippers" teachers: Tracie Morrison, Gerry Gilmartin, Marilyn French, Kaye Stephan, Vicki Mitchell, and Jane Smith; Kevin Christian and Miki Lake for invaluable assistance on photographic shoots; Sussex Down Therapies for their pool.

Designed by Rita Storey.
Edited by Jane Walker.
Editorial Director: Elinor Bagenal
Production Manager: Susan Sutterby
Production Controller: Claire Legg

Printed and bound in Singapore
for Imago.

British Library Cataloguing in Publication data available.
Library of Congress Cataloging in Publication data available.

ISBN 1 902618 51 3

WATER BABY!

A first fun book of water skills

by Lauren Heston   Photography by Zena Holloway

ε

ELEMENT CHILDREN'S BOOKS

SHAFTESBURY, DORSET . BOSTON, MASSACHUSETTS . MELBOURNE, VICTORIA

Contents

Foreword

I have personal reasons to love WATER BABY! It is reminiscent of the special atmosphere I experienced when visiting Lauren and her happy babies. We must be grateful to Lauren Heston and Zena Holloway for demonstrating in a simple and eloquent way how confident babies can be in water. Thanks to such observers of human nature we realize that, until a certain age, young human beings are like all other mammals: they can safely move underwater in the most instinctive way.

Dr. Michel Odent

Introduction

When babies arrive for my classes, only a few weeks old and unable even to hold their heads up, they appear to be totally dependent on others to meet their every need. But once in the water they acquire a new independence — and become really athletic. You only have to look at the amazing photographs in this book to see the enjoyment and tranquility that the babies themselves experience. After many years of teaching, I am still so amazed by the abilities of each tiny child when given the chance to display them. Water provides such a liberating environment for babies. They become truly empowered.

This simple introduction to water skills is designed for babies up to 1 year of age. It brings a fun approach to the teaching of essential life-saving skills. Through this book, I hope that you too will capture this joy.

Lauren Heston

It's good for your baby!

Each year, too many babies and young children die in water-related incidents. The aim of the WATER BABY! program is to try to give your child a fighting chance to survive in the event of an accident.

This program will help you to teach basic safety skills to even the youngest baby. In time, it will give your baby the confidence to back float unaided, and the skill to kick up to the surface, turn round in the water, and hold onto the nearest object.

The exercises in WATER BABY! also introduce your baby to the benefits of an active lifestyle, such as stronger heart and lungs, and improved general health. The program also leads to greater mental alertness and improved coordination in the early years.

By starting the WATER BABY! program, you and your baby are launching out on an adventure. This will be a wonderful shared experience for you both, building further on the bond of love and trust that exists between you. And the time you spend together in the water will help you and your baby to develop a mutual sense of fun.

Why are water skills good for your baby?

Teaching water safety skills to babies from a very young age will:
- equip baby with vital life-saving skills;
- build up baby's heart and lungs;
- improve strength and stamina;
- encourage agility and coordination;
- help baby to relax;
- stimulate awareness and alertness;
- help baby to be more confident;
- strengthen the bond between parent and baby.

SAFETY FIRST!
Never allow your baby to be alone or unsupervised near water. Although this program is designed to teach remarkable water skills, your baby is still far too young to appreciate the dangers of water.

Advice for parents

Before you begin working through this program in the water, make sure you read through each step carefully. Do the bathtime exercises (page 11) before your first visit to the pool. You should always start each pool session with the warm-up routine (page 17). Remember that your baby needs adequate recovery time between submersions. Be alert to signs that your baby is tired – 20 minutes of exercise is usually enough for even the fittest baby.

Your own attitude toward the water safety program in WATER BABY! is the most important ingredient for success. A relaxed and positive approach will give your baby confidence in the water, but if you are feeling anxious and nervous he or she will detect these feelings. If you are worried about being alone in water with your baby, ask a friend to help you work through the steps of this program. Use a clear, strong tone of voice when giving the commands. When doing the exercises, carry out the movements gently but firmly.

Telephone your local swimming pool to check the water temperature before your first visit. Babies hate cold water, and a first session in a cold pool will put them off immediately. For newborns, the temperature should be at least 92° Fahrenheit (33° Celsius), while babies over 6 months will usually tolerate a slightly lower temperature.

Don't be over-ambitious for your baby. This program is intended to be a fun introduction to water skills. On each visit to the pool, try to strike a balance between water play and practicing the exercises described in the various steps.

The WATER BABY! program is designed to span a period of about 9 months involving weekly visits to the pool. Each exercise builds on the previous ones so that your baby's strength and stamina can gradually develop and improve. The steps should be introduced in order. If you have a long break away from the pool, possibly due to illness, your baby will not be as strong in the water as before. If this happens, go back a few steps in the program when you start your visits to the pool again.

Babies – and their parents – benefit enormously from group sessions in the water. There are several specialist teachers who provide infant water safety training programs. Alternatively, your local swimming pool may run organized parent and baby swimming classes that you could join.

STEP 1

In the bath

It is never too soon to introduce your baby to water, and you will feel him relax when you cuddle him in the bath. Do not attempt these exercises alone – you need another person to hand baby to you in the bath. Use a non-slip mat in the bath for extra security. Make sure that the water is deep enough so that baby's legs and back cannot touch the bottom when floating. Remember to check the water temperature. Now warm up the bathroom, have cosy towels ready, and prepare to share the adventure!

The first exercise develops back floating skills. Lie baby's back against your chest. Gently cup his head in the palms of your hands, fingers pointing downward. Do not support baby's neck or back. Make sure his ears are submerged. Supporting baby's head, push him forward into the floating position.

The second exercise introduces word association. Holding baby upright in the crook of your arm, give the command "Ready go!" and swiftly scoop a small amount of water over the top of his head. Do this several times. As baby's confidence grows, pour more water over his head with each command.

◀ Lie baby's back against your chest. Gently cup his head in the palms of your hands, with fingers pointing downward. Do not support baby's neck or back.

▲ Supporting baby's head, push him forward into the floating position. Baby's natural buoyancy will hold his head and body in a horizontal position.

"Ready go!"

◀ Hold baby upright in the crook of your arm. On the command "Ready go!" scoop a small amount of water over the top of baby's head so that it trickles down his face.

11

STEP 2

First visit to the pool

On the first visit, your baby needs time to acclimatize to her new surroundings. Wrapping her in a towel, walk around the pool area for a while. When baby seems relaxed, get into the pool letting the water gently rise up her body. Holding her close to your chest, speak to her reassuringly. If you both feel relaxed and confident, try the two holding positions.

For position 1, place your fingers across baby's chest and your thumbs on her shoulder blades. Hold her to your side, in line with your waist. Hold very young babies more upright; older ones should have their legs out behind. For position 2, place your thumbs over baby's shoulders. Cup her chest with your fingers. Stretch out your arms and walk slowly backward, swaying baby gently from side to side to encourage leg kicking.

When you have mastered these positions, try "reaching." It helps to develop hand–eye coordination. Throw a bathtime toy a few feet in front of baby, splashing to catch her attention. Using position 1, slowly move toward the toy giving the command "Reach!" Don't be discouraged if she does not reach for the toy at first.

◀ With baby's back toward you, place your fingers across her chest and your thumbs on her shoulder blades. Hold her out to your side, in line with your waist.

Holding position 1

Holding position 2

▲ Place thumbs over the top of baby's shoulders, cupping her chest with your fingers. Stretch out your arms and walk back slowly, swaying baby from side to side.

◀ Throw toy in front of baby, while making a splash. Using holding position 1, move slowly toward the toy giving the command "Reach!"

"Reach!"

Step 3

Back floating and splashing

Back floating is a very important skill that will eventually enable your baby to surface and float on his back if there is nothing in the water to hold onto. Practice this exercise with your baby as early as possible. An older baby might struggle when back floating. If so, try moving through the water faster, making the exercise into a game.

Stand with your back against the poolside. Raise one knee and sit baby on it with his back toward you. Cup his head in your hands. Slowly lower your knee while pushing baby out into a back float. When you feel confident, walk slowly backward swaying him from side to side. To stay in a back float baby needs to look straight upward. His ears should be submerged. Hold his attention by looking down into his face. After several weeks, when baby begins to relax in this position, remove one hand, and later both hands.

For the splashing exercise, sit baby on the poolside, holding him under the arms with your arms outstretched. Lift him up before splashing him into the water while giving the command "Ready splash!" Walk backward bouncing baby in and out of the water, repeating the word "Splash!" each time he enters the water.

◀ Stand with your back against the side of the pool. Bring one knee up and sit baby on it with his back toward you. Cup his head in the palms of your hands.

▲ Lower your raised knee slowly, at the same time pushing baby out into the back floating position. Later, move away from the poolside and walk slowly backward, swaying baby from side to side.

"Ready splash!"

◀ Sit baby on the poolside, holding him under the arms with your arms outstretched. Lift him up into the air, give the command "Ready splash!" and bounce him into the water and back out again.

STEP 4

Hold on and turn

This exercise teaches your baby to turn underwater, kick up to the surface, and hold onto the nearest object. Using holding position 1 (page 13), give the command "Hold on!" and draw baby toward the side of the pool. Rest his hands on the rail or wall to encourage him to hold on. A very young baby may not be able to grip, but will benefit from repeating the exercise. As baby's strength develops, let go of his body briefly to allow him to take his own weight.

Next, give the command "Turn!" as you turn baby away from the poolside. At the other side, repeat the commands and actions for "Hold on!" and "Turn!" Repeat this exercise at least six times each time you visit the pool.

You can introduce a play element for baby as well. Holding baby in position 1, give the command "Kick! Kick! Kick!" repeatedly in a sing-song voice as you move across the pool. At the other side, repeat the commands and actions for "Hold on!" and "Turn!" Try to repeat this exercise several times during each visit to the pool.

◄ Using holding position 1 (page 13), give the command "Hold on!" and pull baby toward the rail or pool wall. Rest his hands on the rail or wall to encourage him to hold on.

"Hold on!"

"Turn!"

► Holding baby in position 1, give the command "Turn!" as you turn baby away from the side of the pool.

► Holding baby in position 1, give the command "Kick! Kick! Kick!" repeatedly in a sing-song voice as you move across the pool.

"Kick! Kick! Kick!"

STEP 5

First underwater swim

This is baby's "big day" when she does her first underwater swim. Most parents have mixed emotions about this exercise when they do it for the first time. Don't worry! Your baby may well be surprised by the new experience but she will be in no danger. Try to be relaxed and positive. Take a few slow, deep breaths; don't rush the exercise; give plenty of smiles and encouragement afterward.

To prepare baby for her first submersion, finish the warm-up exercises (page 17) by giving the command "Ready go!" a couple of times, pouring water over baby's head. Now stand with your back against the poolside, with the water at chest height. Hold baby in position 2 (page 13) at arm's length, making eye contact with her.

Giving the command "Ready go!" move baby downward about 6 inches (15 cm) below the water's surface, without bending your arms. Make sure she is fully submerged for a brief moment (her natural buoyancy will offer some resistance). Calmly draw baby toward you and up out of the water into a reassuring cuddle. If baby continues to hold her breath, bounce her up and down gently and blow lightly in her face.

▲ Stand with your back to the poolside, with the water up to chest height. Hold baby at arm's length, using holding position 2 (page 13).

"Ready go!"

▲ Giving the command "Ready go!" at the same time move baby about 6 inches (15 cm) below the water's surface. Make sure she is fully submerged.

◀ Draw baby toward you and back up out of the water into a reassuring cuddle. If she continues to hold her breath, bounce her up and down gently and blow in her face.

STEP 6

Swim off the side

The exercise in this step will help to strengthen your baby's respiratory system over time. Sit baby on the side of the pool, in the same position as for "Ready splash!" (page 15). Next, give the command "Ready go!" in a clear, authoritative tone of voice as you lift him up off the side. Immediately after the command, submerge baby with a firm and fluid action, taking a step backward at the same time. Baby's head should be at least 6 inches (15 cm) below the water's surface.

As you step back, draw baby through the water and up out again, greeting him with a hug and a smile as he surfaces. He should only be submerged for a moment. A few reassuring words, and maybe a handclap for an older baby, will distract the surprised child. If baby continues to hold his breath, which is not unusual, bounce him up and down gently and blow lightly in his face.

You can increase the length of time baby spends underwater as his strength and confidence develop. As his parent, you will instinctively know when he is tired and it's time to stop.

◀ Sit baby on side of pool, in same position as for "Ready splash!" (page 15). As you give the command "Ready go!" lift baby up off the side.

▲ Submerge baby with a firm and smooth action, taking a step back at the same time. Pull baby through the water.

◀ Bring baby up out of the water, giving him a hug as he surfaces. He should only be submerged for a moment. If he is still holding his breath, blow lightly on his face.

STEP 7

Underwater swim unaided

"Ready go!"

◄ Holding baby in position 1 (page 13), face the middle of the pool. Give the command "Ready go!" and submerge baby in one swift movement.

Always remember to start each pool session with a few minutes of warm-up exercises for baby. Follow the exercises described in Step 4 (page 17).

In Step 7, baby will swim underwater without help when you let go of her for a brief moment. Watch her enjoy this new-found freedom! Holding baby in position 1 (page 13), stand facing the middle of the pool. Give the command "Ready go!" and submerge baby in one swift movement. Gently propel her forward through the water before releasing your hands for 1 or 2 seconds.

As baby kicks back up to the surface, calmly lift her out of the water. Give her a reassuring cuddle and lots of praise. Do this exercise at a calm and gentle pace. Avoid any sudden jerky movements as these may startle your baby. If baby begins to surface into a back floating position, encourage this by gently supporting her head. Practice this underwater swim for several visits before moving on to Step 8.

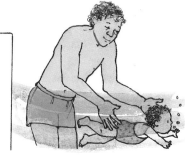

▲ Gently propel baby through the water. Then release your hands from her body for 1 or 2 seconds.

▲ As baby kicks back up to the surface, calmly lift her out of the water. Give baby a cuddle and lots of praise.

STEP 8

Learning to breathe

Your baby will learn two new safety skills in this step. In the first exercise, baby learns to hold onto anything within reach after a submersion. In the second exercise, he learns to take a breath whenever possible.

Holding baby in position 1 (page 13), stand about 3 feet (1 meter) from the poolside. Giving the command "Ready go!" submerge her in a swimming position and step forward. When you reach the side, give the command "Hold on!" as baby surfaces. Lift her up so that she can grasp the rail or pool wall, guiding her hands if necessary. If your baby is older and stronger, allow her to swim freely towards the poolside as described in Step 7 (page 23).

For the second exercise, hold baby in position 2 (page 13) and make eye contact. Giving the command "Ready go!" submerge baby and simultaneously take a small step backward. As you bring baby to the surface, give the command "Breathe!" allowing a moment for her to take a breath. Give the command "Go!" and repeat the exercise a second time. As baby grows stronger, increase the number of times that she takes a breath.

"Ready go!"

▲ Holding baby in position 2 (page 13), make eye contact with her. Give the command "Ready go!" and submerge baby, taking a step backward at the same time.

"Breathe!"

▲ Bring baby back to the surface and up out of the water, giving the command "Breathe!" Allow her time to take a breath.

"Go!"

▲ Now repeat the exercise, giving the command "Go!" Increase the number of times that baby takes a breath as her strength develops.

Step 9

Underwater turn

This next safety skill aims to teach baby how to turn underwater and make his way back to the side of the pool. It starts with a game so that you can practice helping baby to turn on the water's surface.

Hold baby upright in the water at arm's length, with his back toward you. Now twist him round to the right, giving the command "Turn!" at the same time. As you twist him round to the left, repeat the command. Do this exercise several times – baby will love it if you play a game of peek-a-boo at the same time.

The next stage moves on to making a turn underwater. Hold baby in the same position as above. Now lift him up high out of the water and give the command "Ready go! Turn!" Submerge baby at least 6 inches (15 cm) below the water's surface and let go of him. Encourage him to turn back toward you by immediately giving his hips a gentle swivel. (With practice, a 1-year-old baby will be strong enough to turn by himself.) Lift baby out of the water facing you, and once again give him plenty of praise – this is a demanding exercise.

◀ Hold baby upright, at arm's length, with his back toward you. Give the command "Turn!" as you twist him round to the right. Repeat as you twist him to the left.

"Turn!"

▶ Hold baby in the same position as above and lift him up high out of the water. Give the command "Ready go! Turn!" and submerge baby at least 6 inches (15 cm) below the water. Then let go of him.

"Ready go! Turn!"

◀ Help baby to turn back toward you by immediately giving his hips a gentle swivel. Lift him out of the water facing you, and give him lots of praise.

STEP 10

Walk back and let go

This is a fun exercise that allows baby to have a free swim – and with a feeling of speed. By creating currents in the water you will encourage her to kick. In a busy public pool, make sure you give yourself plenty of space to do this exercise!

Hold baby in position 2 (page 13), with your arms outstretched and baby's legs floating out behind her. Take several steps backward to build up a current in the space between you and baby. Give the command "Ready go!" and submerge her as you continue to move backward. Release baby at arm's length and let the water carry her toward you as you keep walking back.

The next exercise works best if you are confident when floating on your back. If you don't feel confident, get a friend to stand close by and help you. Stand facing the side of the pool, holding baby's back against your chest. Lean back into a floating position and push off lightly from the side with your feet. Hold baby in place with one hand across her tummy, and kick your legs gently to stay afloat. An older baby can sit up on your chest and face toward you.

"Ready go!"

▲ Holding baby in position 2 (page 13), take several steps back to build up a current. Give the command "Ready go!" and submerge baby. Release her at arm's length, letting the water carry her back toward you.

Floating

▲ Stand facing the poolside, holding baby's back against your chest. Lean back into a floating position and push off lightly from the side with your feet.

▲ Kick your legs gently to stay afloat. Hold baby in place with one hand across her tummy.

STEP 11

Belly flop into the water

This exercise gets your baby used to the shock of hitting the water with more force than previously. (Remember that no one may be on hand to give commands or break his fall if he drops into water accidentally.) Make sure that the pool is deep enough to do this exercise safely. You need another adult with you to lift baby up as he surfaces.

Sit on the side of the pool with your feet in the water, and baby sitting between your legs. The second adult should stand in the water about 4 feet (1.25 meters) away. Hold baby out in the "belly flop" position about 6 inches (15 cm) above the water. Give the command "Ready go!" louder than usual, as baby is facing away from you and might be distracted, and let go of him.

Allow baby a few seconds to begin surfacing before the other adult gently lifts him out of the water. Get into the water yourself to give extra reassurance to a surprised baby. If he appears to be surfacing into a back floating position this is very good – simply support his head as in the bathtime exercise (page 11).

▲ Sit on the poolside with your feet in the water, and baby sitting between your legs. Another adult should stand in the water about 4 feet (1.25 meters) away.

"Ready go!"

▲ Hold baby out in the "belly flop" position about 6 inches (15 cm) above the water. Give the command "Ready go!" in a loud voice and let go of him.

▲ Once underwater, allow baby a few seconds to begin surfacing before the other adult steps in and gently lifts him out of the water.

STEP 12

Drop in and turn back

The exercise that you will be doing in this step is based on the "Hold on! Turn!" skill described in Step 4 (page 17). The exercise creates a more lifelike situation, developing the skills learned earlier. It aims to teach your baby, if she should fall into the water by accident, to turn back to the side automatically, kick up to the surface, and hold onto the nearest available object.

Once again, you will need the help of a second adult who should start the exercise standing in the water, facing away from the side of the pool. Sit on the poolside with your legs in the water. Hold baby out to your side in an upright position, with her toes just touching the water. Give the command "Ready go! Turn!" and let go of baby.

Once she is fully submerged below the surface, the second adult can then help baby to turn back to the side by gently twisting her hips. As baby's head surfaces, give the command "Hold on!" The other adult can guide baby's hands toward the rail or wall of the pool if necessary.

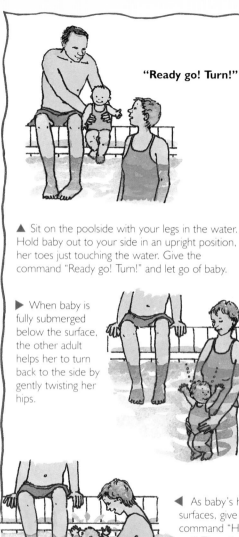

"Ready go! Turn!"

▲ Sit on the poolside with your legs in the water. Hold baby out to your side in an upright position, her toes just touching the water. Give the command "Ready go! Turn!" and let go of baby.

▶ When baby is fully submerged below the surface, the other adult helps her to turn back to the side by gently twisting her hips.

◀ As baby's head surfaces, give the command "Hold on!" The other adult can guide baby's hands toward the rail or wall if necessary.

"Hold on!"

STEP 13

Belly flop and swim to side

This exercise combines the basic safety skills of a belly flop, taking a breath on surfacing, and holding on. They form one continuous exercise for the older, fitter baby. As always, remember to do your warm-up routine first, but don't wait until the end of your pool visit to do a demanding exercise such as this one.

You need the help of another adult who should sit on the poolside. He or she holds the baby out in the belly flop position, as in Step 11 (page 31). You should stand in the water – to the side of the baby – and give the command "Ready go!" As baby is dropped into the pool, step forward to help her surface using holding position 1 (page 13) out to your side.

When baby's head is clear of the water, give the command "Breathe! Go!" and submerge her fully while stepping forward. Repeat this breathing exercise once more. When you are both about 3 feet (1 meter) away from the opposite side of the pool, again give the command "Breathe! Go!" but this time allow baby a free swim to the side. As she nears the side, help her to reach up while giving the command "Hold on!"

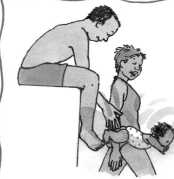

◀ The other adult sits on the poolside and holds baby out over the water in the belly flop position.

"Ready go!"

◀ Stand in the water to the side of baby and give the command "Ready go!" As baby drops into the pool, step forward to help her surface.

"Breathe! Go!"

◀ Hold baby in position 1 out to your side. When her head is clear of the water, give the command "Breathe! Go!" and submerge her fully while stepping forward. Repeat this breathing exercise one more time.

STEP 14

The first dive

This exercise has been included because babies adore its boisterous nature. Also, it serves as an early preparation for the more conventional swimming skills that your child will learn when older. Later on, toddlers will enjoy diving for toys placed on the bottom of the pool, or diving down through a parent's legs.

Hold baby by the arm and leg farthest away from you, supporting his weight on your forearms. Next, give the command "Ready go! Dive!" Lift baby's legs higher than his head and submerge him with a rapid, fluid movement. At the lowest point of his dive, release baby into a free swim underwater and allow him to kick back up to the surface.

Practice this exercise for a few weeks. Once baby grows used to the technique, hold him in position 1 (page 13) when he surfaces and take him to the side to give the command "Hold on!" This sequence encourages the development of a safety skill that your baby will eventually carry out automatically.

◀ Stand in the water and hold baby by the arm and leg farthest away from you. Support his weight on your forearms.

◀ Give the command "Ready go! Dive!" and lift baby's legs higher than his head. Submerge him with a rapid, fluid movement.

"Ready go! Dive!"

◀ At the lowest point of the dive, release baby and let him swim freely underwater. Allow him to kick back up to the surface.

STEP 15

On the bottom of the pool

It is great fun to sit on the bottom of the pool with your baby – really enjoy sharing this underwater experience! Try wearing a pair of goggles or a diving mask so that you can watch baby's expression. This can also be a lovely, gentle exercise to do if your baby has lost confidence underwater – this often happens around the first birthday. In such cases, try to hold baby in a relaxed manner. Always remember to support the back of a younger baby's head.

Cradle baby in an upright position and bounce up and down in the water several times. Give the command "Ready go!" in a strong voice, and submerge together while fully bending your legs into a kneeling position. Rest on the bottom for a second before resurfacing. If you breathe out slightly when underwater this will help you to submerge more easily.

Over time you will be able to stay underwater for longer. This exercise helps your baby's physical strength and confidence to grow. Once on the bottom of the pool, have some fun: draw baby toward you until you are face to face and then rub noses, pull faces at each other, or kiss!

◀ Cradle baby in an upright position and bounce up and down in the water several times.

▶ Give the command "Ready go!" in a strong voice. Submerge together, fully bending your legs into a kneeling position.

"Ready go!"

▶ Rest on the bottom of the pool for a second before resurfacing. Try rubbing noses with baby, or giving him a kiss.

39

 # Having fun

The world of water adds a whole new dimension to your baby's play – and she will learn quickly when having fun. When you visit the pool, take along her favorite bathtime toys – familiar objects will help to build her confidence. Alternatively, find new, brightly colored toys with an interesting movement to stimulate her. Taking older children with you on a pool visit will inspire baby to try new water skills with greater confidence.

Water play with other babies introduces early social skills. Babies love pushing a large beach ball to each other, or having it bounced off their heads. These activities are not only fun, but also help to develop your baby's coordination at the same time.

Sometimes your baby may not enjoy the exercises as much as usual, so try to include elements of the exercises in your water games. Maybe an underwater swim up to a toy sitting on the poolside might appeal more today. You can also have fun by replacing the usual commands with favorite nursery rhymes and songs: "Humpty Dumpty sat on a wall. Humpty Dumpty had a great fall!" prepares baby for a big splash in the water.

 # More fun!

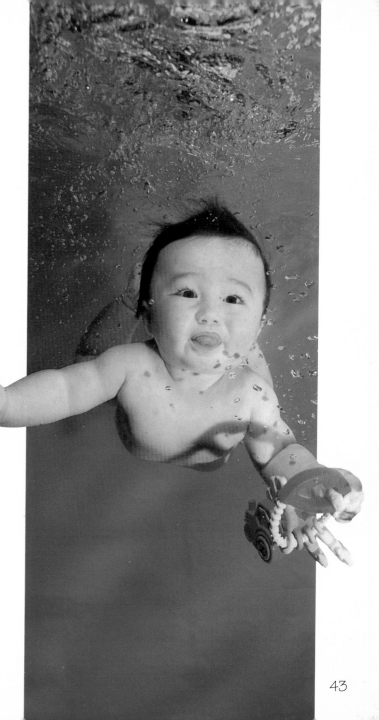

Always make sure that your visits to the pool remain fun for your baby. By including plenty of play in each session you will ensure that the enjoyment of water stays with your baby for life, alongside the skills he has learned to stay safe.

Older babies always enjoy swimming through a colored hoop or diving for a weighted toy. A swim through a parent's legs appeals to a young child's sense of humor! Be prepared to join in the play yourself. Surprise your baby by popping up from underwater with a "Boo!" or jumping into the water with your toddler.

Older babies who can walk often make up their own games by climbing out of the pool and immediately launching themselves back into your arms. Always make sure that baby jumps well clear of the steps or poolside rail.

If you are a confident swimmer, you can take baby for a ride on your back or tummy. Babies love joining in these water games with you. Finally, an underwater dive together from the surface is a very special experience to share with your baby.

Answers to your questions

How long will it take to complete the WATER BABY! program?

The whole program should take about 9 months to complete. But don't try to hurry it – there are no shortcuts to developing your baby's strength and stamina. You should repeat each step on several visits to the pool before progressing to the next one.

I can't swim, so how can I do this program with my baby?

In this case, you should only take baby in the water in a supervised pool. However, it's not your own ability in the water that is important – it's your attitude. You can do all these exercises in shallow water where you will be able to stand at all times. Take a swimming friend with you for added confidence.

My 1-year-old used to love going to the pool but now he cries every time. What should I do?

Young children often go through a phase where they no longer seem to enjoy the water as much as before. Don't be put off. Continue your regular visits to the pool, but don't undo all the earlier good work by forcing your baby to do the exercises. If necessary just play in the water, and baby's confidence will shortly return.

My baby suffers from asthma. Is it safe for him to go swimming?

Exercise-induced asthma is almost unknown among swimmers as the air they breathe in the pool area is warm and humid. The exercises in this program will help to strengthen your baby's heart and lungs. However, if your baby's condition gives you any cause for concern, always consult a health professional.

How will my baby know not to breathe in when underwater?

A basic response known as the "diving reflex" is present in all of us, but is much more active in babies. It will cause your baby to hold her breath automatically when underwater.

At what age can I start taking my baby to the pool?

Newborn babies cannot regulate their own body temperature and so they should not be allowed to get cold. However, you can visit a swimming pool heated to 92° Fahrenheit (33° Celsius) or above as soon as you feel comfortable and confident about doing so. Babies over 6 months of age will usually tolerate a lower water temperature and you can take them to your local swimming pool.

If you have any specific concerns, consult a health professional for advice.

Should my baby wear armbands?

No. The exercises in WATER BABY! are designed to develop baby's natural response in the water. Wearing armbands will give her a false sense of security. You will be with her at all times to give her the necessary support.

What should my baby wear in the pool?

Colorful waterproof swim diapers (nappies) are available for babies. They will contain any embarrassing accidents when in the water. Do not use disposable diapers in the water as they become waterlogged and will disintegrate.

This book is for all the "Little Dippers" past, present, and future – for their inspiration and hope.

45